Walking with The Devil

THE TASTE OF HATE

WALKING WITH THE DEVIL

This is a story of a little girl's darkness

Cover Designer: Blu Lloyd

Author: T. HARRIS

REVISED SECOND EDITION

T. HARRIS

PO BOX 70893

BROOKLYN NY 11207 USA

PUBLISHING HISTORY

Original copyright 2014 by T. Harris

Copyright 2015

Library of Congress Cataloging-in-Publication

All right reserved. No part of this book may be reproduced or transmitted in any form or by any means, electronic or mechanical. Including photocopying, or by any information storage or retrieval system without permission.

ISBN: 9780692284711

Published in The United States

The Taste of Hate

CONTENT

INTRODUCTION

CHAPTER 1 - The Beginning

CHAPTER 2 – Sundays

CHAPTER 3 - Uncle Sam Changes

CHAPTER 4 - The Hospital

CHAPTER 5 - Back at the House

CHAPTER 6 – Angry

CHAPTER 7 – My Aunt Sissy

CHAPTER 8 - The Seduction

CHAPTER 9 – The Taste of Hate

INTRODUCTION

I awake one morning, with the feeling of a swollen tongue. A tongue feeling too large for my mouth. Topped with the ruggedness of hard coarse sandpaper coated with hot burning sand straight from the Sahara Desert. As I glided the tip of my tongue across the roof of my mouth from back, to the front, and gently down the back of my front teeth. I felt my tongue, slit in two, as if it was a fork in the road and each of those slits were split in two tails. As my tongue left passing my lips, I heard the same sounds in my head every day, of snakes rattling and hissing until.

Chapter 1

The Beginning

Hey I have some things to get off my chest, and I need you to please listen. I have been carrying these memories around with me all my life. Sharing them with no one. I'm at the point where I can't keep them to myself anymore. "It's just driving me so crazy." So today I choose you. "Yes you" I choose you because I was told, you are the best listener in town. So here it goes. By the way my name is Hattie Mae. I was named after my great Grandmother, my Grandmother's mother. And my Grandfather's name is James.

It all started the summer of 1966, I was eight years old. Every summer, like every other kid in the north, we got shipped out to the south for A "quote unquote summer vacation," until we became skillful enough to cry on cue on our knees, with our hands tightly gripping the circulation out of our prayer like hands, trying to convince our parent or parents, that we are responsible enough to take care of just ourselves or all of our younger siblings. My cousin's and I usually got sent to our Granddaddy's house. This time I went south alone. "Only if I knew"

My Grandfather was a very distinguish man, a man who served his country and survived with physical life time injuries. He was a World War Two Veteran. He was one of the finest musician's I have ever known. Gramps was a peaceful man, quiet, calm, and full of insightful wisdom. Gramps was also a heavy drinker, and a gambler. Oh! "The hell with it", truth be told he was a drunk. He said my Grandmother drove him to drinking. Well, she might have been responsible for him "NOT" being able to stop drinking. To be honest, we all know it was the results of the war. And yes, he was all the above a great man.

Back in the day people cared what other people thought of them. They had a sense of proudness about themselves. My Grandfather was a very well dressed man. Every day he was clean shaven, haircut, white crispy shirt ties or no tie, hat and his shoes were never dull. He and I would spend an hour every night spit shinning his shoes and chewing the fat or you can say sit and talk. My Gramps had all the answers to my questions. "And boy did I ever have a bunch of questions.

"OH! Did I mention he was soft spoken? There is nothing like getting into trouble and have my Gramps" just look at you and never ever, letting you know how pissed he is." He would calmly look at me, and calmly speak to me in the most annoying tone. Let's face it." I'm from Brooklyn." I don't need you to talk to me, starring me in my face,"" looking into my eyes" and calmly giving me a behavioral analysis.'" "Not for a whole hour." "ARE YOU KIDDING ME.?" I'm eight years old, shit!! "Just beat me."

I even offered to go outside and get my own switch. Because that's what we do back home in the hood. You do something; you get your ass beat. End of story! "HEY GRAMPS WHERE IS THE BELT? I'm running through the house looking for something that he can spank me with, because his talking to me is driving me in sane. "HOW ABOUT I GO GET A SWITCH OR A TREE BRANCH"? "HEY GRAMPS DO YOU HEAR ME. "HEY! I FOUND SOME RAW HIDE STAPS," "WILL THAT DO"?

"Man oh man" I remember that walk to the shoe shop around the corner from my house in Brooklyn. I had to get my own raw hide straps. That walk got longer and longer, every single day I had to go.

"Oh yeah," I was a challenging kid. Not bad, I just had this thing about authority. I challenged it no matter where it came from, and whomever delivered it. It was a family trait. I was taught by my Grandmother and Grandfather. I guess it was because of the times they grew up in, early, early, nineteen hundreds. They were true gladiators in their own time.

So anyway back to Gramps, I'm crying, my shirt is wet, my knees hurt from kneeling on them for such a longtime, like an hour. My Gramps had me on my knees, begging him and Jesus. "Please Gramps just beat me," "Lord Jesus please make him stop talking to me, oh lord help me". "Gramps I'll go get the switch." "Please just punish me." "Please let's just get this over already"!

He quietly said to me. "You don't know how to listen." I stopped crying and I looked up at my Grandfather and said, "What"? I "don't listen" I brought my voice down, "Gramps I been listening to you for an hour," I said to him, "I'm sorry! "All I did was eat some donuts." And he kept repeating it over and over, at least four times. "You don't listen." "You don't know how to listen." "You need to learn" "how to listen," "and follow directions." He then said to me, I know I taught you how to question those that make demands of you. "You need to learn

how to listen," and learn the difference between a demand and a direction.

I sat on the floor because by now my knees were killing me. I sat down and said to myself, maybe I need to shut up and get this action over with. I never thought in a million years at that time, I was about to learn something. I still didn't catch on until I became an adult. What can I say, I was a stupid kid.

The one thing that truly stuck with me was this quote. "IN ORDER TO BE A GREAT LEADER, YOU MUST FIRST LEARN HOW TO FOLLOW." My Gramps was well spoken and ahead of his time.

Chapter 2

SUNDAY'S

Yeah! My Gramps was a charmer, good looking and all that. Six feet one inch's tall light skinned with jet black curly hair. His mother was white and his father was black, and no he didn't come from a broken home. He's parents was a married Biracial couple with ten biracial kids. Oh my God". That's another story.

Every Sunday we went to church, and every Sunday the church ladies where like floozies, "Hey Brother James" "Good Morning Brother James" I would watch them bat their eyes, wink at him, rub his back, his arms. "Believe me, it was too much for my young eyes."

Back then the liquor stores never opened on Sunday's and never before 11 AM on any given day during the week. Now days the liquor stores are open before you wake up and roll out the bed in the morning. That just killed all the business for the bootleggers. I remember going to the bootleggers every Sunday morning after church.

The crew, which was a bunch of my Grandfather's friends. Would show up to the house too drink and gamble. They would play cards in the dining room and shoot a game of craps (dice) on the living room floor. The house would be so dark," I felt like a bat with no wings. The heavy drapery would be drawn so tight; you couldn't see your hands in front of your face. I felt as if we were in a cave. The lamps only had a high wattage of twenty-five. It was almost blinding when I went to play in the fabulously evenly layered cement yard.

I remember when I would sneak a peek out of my bedroom window. Just keep in mind my bedroom is on the second floor. The blinds would be closed from the basement to the second floor. And trust me no one was allowed to look out the window, I mean no one. Not even his guest. Not even his best friend Uncle Sam of forty years.

I called him Uncle Sam, he's not my real Uncle. I wished I could have called him Shit Face. And if I needed to be polite about it, I would have called him Uncle Shit Face. We will get back to him.

So when I took the sneak peek challenge, I got my hind tail reamed a whole new butt hole every time I did it. I always wondered how my Grandfather knew when I was looking out the window. It didn't matter that we were on separate floors.

That's when I learned, when you're in total darkness, and you shed an itty bitty light it changes the contrast of the darkness. Which only meant, my dumb ass should have learned how to close the door and put a towel down at the bottom of it. So the itty bitty sunlight wouldn't seep through the crack, when one is trying to be sneaky, and catch a little light. I should have made sure, the door didn't squeak or make noise while closing it because, "I tell you my Grand Pa didn't have big ears for nothing." "Man oh Man" "he saw and heard everything."

Let's get back to Uncle Sam. Hum! Wow! What a character. Every pay check this man ever made went to gambling. Everyone had to pay the house and the house was my Grandfather. If you got ugly or had ugly guess show up to the house, you got put out. Even Uncle Sam got the boot.

Every Sunday I was surrounded by the quietest, drunks I had ever met in my life. If you got to loud you would hear my Gramps whisper, "PISTTT"!! Hush! "My neighbors might hear you," "now Hush up! (In a quiet but stern voice)

The Taste of Hate

My Grandfather lived on a tree lined block with all attached private houses. Houses were lined up on both sides of the street. Everybody knew everybody, I mean by their first name and nick name. Not just by face, they knew your whole family. They know where you been, where you came from and where you were going. Shaking my head. I thought they were just being nosey, silly me.

Uncle Sam had a wife name Delores. Well let me tell you really quick about Miss Delores. "She was one ass kicking momma." I guess that was because she had a very scary boyfriend. AKA cousin, because she was married. No one knew his name. He would drive Miss Delores to my Grandfather's house whenever she thought Uncle Sam was drinking, and losing his money to the house. Which was true and "Yes," That would be to Grandpa and his house.

I will never forget Miss Delores would show up every Sunday afternoon in a black 1966 Convertible Lincoln Continental with Suicide

Doors driven by her aka cousin. He just had that evil look. The look that would cut your eyes out, if you made direct eye contact with him.

Uncle Sam would hear the car pull up and say "Brother please tell her I'm not here." Miss Delores would get out of the car and start screaming out Sam's name. "SAM!! SAM!!! BRING YOUR DUMB ASS OUT HERE"!

"Oh My God," "Miss Delores did not like my Grandfather," and she never stepped foot on the porch. So of course, being that my Grandfather wanted to keep things quiet and under cover, you know on the down low. Uncle Sam got put out, and Miss Delores would commence to beat the living shit out of him. She would tare that bald lumpy head up with her pocket book, which we found out later, was full of small rocks. (Laughing out loud until my stomach hurt) She would beat him until he was on the ground and needed help getting up.

The Taste of Hate

Well needless to say Uncle Sam was out for the count. And the boys had to run out as quick as drunks can run. ("You don't know I'm laughing really hard right now") only if you could have seen what my eyes saw. Ok picture this, three really drunk men trying to hold each other up while walking down three steps. And each of them missing a different step. "Come on you got to admit that's priceless."

Now picture them struggling to pick dead weight off the ground, two hundred and forty pounds of dead weight. "I'm sorry but I'm rolling on the floor right now." While they are trying to get Uncle Sam off the ground. Miss Delores is adding that extra weight pushing him down by digging in his pockets hoping to find some money. But no money is to be found. It's in the house with Gramps.

That poor man was in the street broke and broken. Oh God I wish you can see what's in my head. Still laughing, Please Just take a moment and visualize. The boys had to literally scrape Uncle Sam up off the ground and drag his sorry ass in the house. Well they drug him because they were too drunk to pick him up. (Still laughing)

CHAPTER 3

UNCLE SAM CHANGES HIS PATTERN

My Grandfather always had everyone out of the house by eight pm. And every Sunday everyone left.

Uncle Sam changed his pattern. All of a sudden he started getting to drunk to drive home. I knew he wasn't drunk, tipsy yes, but what can you say to your Grandfather about his best friend faking his drunkenness. "Nothing," "zilch," "not a damn thing."

The Taste of Hate

Whenever he would look at me, he made me feel like slime was pouring down from the sky on to my head sliding down to my feet filling my shoes with sticky goo, icy cold goo. Uncle Sam Changed. I felt like the goo was holding me down to the ground like a two-ton block of dried cement. I was afraid of not knowing what this feeling was. Here I am standing in space with an unknown emotion. Afraid to call for help, trying to scream out loud feeling my words swelling up in my throat, and my words suffocating me until I can feel my eyes bulging out of its sockets, eyes blood shot red, with burning hot sweat pouring down from the top of my head. I'm standing here with tears the size of golf balls, slowly rolling down my cheeks. With a tear soaked shirt still screaming out loud in my head for help. "HELP"!!!! "HELP ME"!! "PLEASE SOMEBODY HELP ME"!

And I remembered a song I had just learned in church the Sunday before leaving New York for the summer. The song is called "Hold to Gods Unchanging Hand" It went like this in my head. "VERY LOUD BECAUSE I WAS

SCREAMING THESE WORDS IN MY HEAD", I WANTED TO MAKE SURE GOD AND EVERYONE ELSE IN THE UNIVERSE HEARD ME". "HERE WE GO."

"HOLD TO HIS HAND," "GODS UNCHANGING HAND," "HOLD TO HIS HAND," "GODS UNCHANGING HAND," "HOLD TO HIS HAND," "GODS UNCHANING HAND," "TRUST HIM, WHO WILL NOT LEAVE YOU WHAT SOEVER.

" That's all I remembered, and just as I finished the words, so ever, in my head, I felt the most ginormous hand in the world lift me off the floor and landed me back on my feet ever so gently. Don't forget I'm a kid. My imagination is huge. That moment was a bundle of "oh shit help me Jesus," "what just happened"? "Thank you lord." "My body froze," I don't think at that moment I was able to blink. My body, my mind, and my spirit felt like I was in a washing machine that quickly gyrated into a never ending spin cycle.

The Taste of Hate

I'm trying to processes everything. I thought I had lost my hearing. There wasn't a sound in the house. I thought I died and was going to heaven.

I saw my Grandfather playing his guitar and blowing his harmonica. Uncle Sam was sitting there singing, clapping and laughing. I'm looking at them and I can't hear a thing. Gramps and Uncle Sam was on the other side of the living room. I still couldn't hear a thing. I laid there on the floor in a fetal position. It was as if, I was in visible to the world. So I just laid there quietly. Now all I hear is my heart beating rapidly, like it's about to punch a hole through my chest and hit the floor.

Then I said in my head. Lord please don't let my heart fall on the floor. I don't know how to clean up blood. If I mess up gramps floor he's going to kill me. "Please lord help me" I just want to go to sleep, and then I felt my heart begin to slow down. It was the most remarkable sound I had ever heard in my little life. Soon the sound of my heart could not be heard anymore, and I began to hear the sweet sound of music being played by my Grandfather, and the sweet sound of laughter coming from my mouth.

I knew then I had that direct line to my lord and savior. That line the old folks was talking and singing about in church. I got up off the floor feeling like someone else. Feeling like I needed to re-introduce me to myself. I didn't quite understand at the time why I was feeling that way. So now I'm getting off the floor. After all is said and done.

We sat down to have dinner. I don't know about your Grandfather, but my gramps knew how to throw down in the (You got to spell it out) "K I T C H E N". Gramps made Code fish, Fried okra, Home Made Butter Milk Biscuits, white rice and gravy. Please don't judge, and stop turning up your nose in discuss, you got to try it first. Until then smile like me, and don't forget a side of lemon aide (homemade)

"Oh Boy, Oh Boy". And my favorite desert, banana pudding. Man! Oh! Man! Did I have a Happy Belly? I'm sitting here right now rubbing my belly and licking my lips. YUMMY! YUMMY! Oh My God. OO! wee!! I'm sorry I just left you for a moment, "my memory is salivating like crazy right now." I wish you were in my head.

So we are sitting at the table right now Uncle Sam is not talking much his face is practically in his plate. His eye balls are rolled up in the back of his head trying to peek at me. This is true talk. He rolled his eyes so far back he gave himself a headache and past out. He fell out of the chair and hit the back his head on the radiator. Now remember he was tipsy. Maybe a little too tipsy, but not drunk. "Sorry "I'm laughing again" After Gramps got Sam off the floor, it looked like Uncle Sam grew another head. Huge bump. Well as you already know. That became a hospital run.

CHAPTER 4

THE HOSPITAL

Gramps called his wife Miss Delores. Remember she don't like my Grandfather, so he tells Miss Delores to hold on, and then he put me on the phone. Now Miss Delores is thinking Gramps called her for Uncle Sam. Now I get on the phone to tell Miss Delores we are taking Uncle Sam to the Hospital. The first thing that comes out of her mouth is, "You stupid son of a bitch", "what the fuck do your drunk ass want now." "If you want me to come get your ass you better have some money! "Now what the fuck do you want"?

I replied in a, frighten and panicky loud voice. "UNCLE SAM IS DEAD, AND WE TAKING HIM TO THE HOSPITAL! And I quickly hung up the phone. "I'm sorry again, I didn't laugh them, but I'm laughing my ass off right now."

The Taste of Hate

By this time Gramps already had Uncle Sam out back and in the car. Blood was all over the place. My Grandfather had the nerve, to tell me to go sit in the back of the car with Uncle Sam. I thought he had lost he's ever loving mind. Uncle Sam's head was bleeding like an open Johnny pump. (For my young people. A Johnny pump is a fire hydrant) Gramps said somebody had to hold the towel on Uncle Sam's bleeding Head. So I get in the back seat of the car with Uncle Sam. Gramps said hold it down and press hard but not too hard. I ask gramps, what happens if I press it to hard? Gramps replied!! Just do what I tell you!

Ok so I'm holding the towel over Uncle Shit Face's head. Next thing I know; I feel his hand rubbing the inside of my thigh. I accidently pressed on the top of his head trying to push myself away from him. My lord this man scream so loud. It scared gramps so bad he slammed on the breaks. Uncle Sam's head went weaving and bobbing all over the place. Uncle Sam keep screaming my neck! my neck!

I was rolling on the floor in the back of the car and laughing all at the same time.

Gramps got out of the car to see if we were ok. He picked me up off the floor and put me in the seat. He asked me why was I laughing so hard. Ok, come in my head. Picture a two-month old baby with no neck support. Can you see it? Can you see the baby's head rolling around in a circle on top of it's the neck? Now picture the baby with no eye control. That was Uncle Shit Face's head. I don't know about you but I'm laughing my ass off right now.

So we get to the hospital. We pull up to the emergency room entrance, and the staff takes Uncle Sam in. Gramps took me to the waiting room, and all you hear is pure hell erupting. Miss Delores is there asking to see her dead husband. Only they can't find him, because one, he's not dead, and two, we just got him to the hospital.

The Taste of Hate

Miss Delores see's my Grandfather and me entering the waiting room. Miss Delores stops and she just stares at Gramps like she wants to say something to him, but was afraid to. The next thing I hear is Miss Delores screaming out loud. "There he goes, that's the son of a bitch that killed my husband" She's crying and falling out all over the place. She was just acting crazy.

So the cops come over to where my Gramps and I were sitting. The cop asks my Gramps. Do you know the lady accusing you of killing her husband? Gramps replied, yes sir I do. Then the cop asked. What can you tell me about her dead husband? My grandfather calmly replied. He's in the emergency room being treated for a head and neck injury. Cop said explain to me what happened. Gramps said. He was at my house he got drunk he fell and hit his head on the radiator.

The other cop went into the emergency room with Miss Delores to identify Uncle Sam. The cop told Gramps to stay put and don't go anywhere. As soon as they left Gramps snatched me up by the arm, we were out, gone like flash. Had me so high off the ground my feet were dangling in the air. We were out quick fast and in a hurry. I couldn't wait to get home.

CHAPTER 5

BACK AT THE HOUSE

"Oh Man" Home at last. I went straight to the tub. 'No for real' when I say I went straight to the tub. I stepped in the tub and sat down with no water and fully dressed. I filled the tub up while I was sitting in it. I was covered in blood, sweat and tears. I smelt bad.

Now it's a new day and it's clean up time. I wished I could have bleached everything Uncle Sam touched. He was just yucky. His lips were just nasty. He had them cigar lips. You know the lips that look like a worn out Vagina, thick and hanging all over his face just

The Taste of Hate

full of lumps and bumps always wet, and his tongue was always sticking out the side of his mouth. "Oh My God," I'm about to throw up. Just thinking about it is making me sick.

The doorbell rings, and my heart drops when I see Uncle Shit Face standing there on the porch looking dirty hungry and smelling like elephant shit. "Man oh man" "did he ever stink," As he got closer he smelled like day old piss soaked in old cigar Tabaco being pushed through a soaked infused alcohol smelling t-shirt, ewe!! "Throw up, yuck!!!!

So after I finished cleaning the kitchen I ask my grandfather may I please air out the house, you know can I please open all the windows and throw out the trash. My Grandfather had a great since of humor. He was elated with the idea of me taking out the trash. He thought the smell was coming from the garbage. Please! Baby girl Please! Whatever that smell is, you have my permission to toss it out. His words not mine.

He said, that smell is just ungodly. I laughed so hard, and that's only because I knew where the smell was coming from.

I told Gramps Uncle Sam needed a bath, it's him that smell bad. So Gramps went to smell Uncle Sam, and was like, Jesus! Christ! Man! "You got to go home and wash your butt" GET OUT! "I can't have you in my house smelling like that." So Uncle Sam left. He went home to wash his long overdue stinking ass and change his clothes. FINALLY, For the first time this summer it was a great day, just me and Gramps. So Gramps starts to play the guitar and blow on his harmonica, and sing some country blues and gospel songs. A couple of days go by and before you knew it. Yes, that's right it's Sunday again.

It was a great day for church. Sunday July 24, 1966. Hot as a burning furnace in the winter time. I will never forget that day as long as I shall ever live. When I got to church I saw people that looked like me, my uncles, my aunts and my other Grandfather. I looked around, "OH MY GOD! MY FAMILY! I met family members that was only talked about. It was family day at the church all members invited their family members. We played laughed, and ate like we were not going to eat tomorrow.

Now it's time to say a sad farewell to all my family not knowing when I will see them again. I was so sad, and just thinking about that day now makes me a little sad. Because some of them I never got to see again. "May God, bless their souls" What a good time we had.

Back to the order of the day. We go to the bootleggers and get the usual. We stop by the store and get the beer a pack of camel's cigarettes no filter. Gramps told me to pick out my snacks and soda pop.

We get to the house. Now Gramps always drives past the front of the house before going around to the back of the house. That's where we park the car. And to our surprise we see Uncle Sam on the porch with a suite case.

So we drove around the back, parked the car in the yard. As we are entering the house Gramps tells me to go open the door for Uncle Sam. Now you should know by now, me letting Uncle Sam in the house was the last thing I wanted to do. So I reluctantly opened the door. And in comes Uncle Shit Face. He has this thing where every time he looks at me he licks his lips like he just finished eating fried chicken and pork chops. He comes in sits down on the sofa near the door with his suite case full of his belongings still outside on the porch.

Gramps is now entering the living room. He is putting the finishing touches on things for his Sunday crew. Gramps say to Sam: "Hey Sam what's going on with the baggage outside?" Uncle Sam say to Gramps. Man! "That crazy ass woman put me out of my own house." "I have nowhere to go" I don't know what to do" (He's crying his heart out) "Delores keeps calling the cops on me."

"My boys came by and told me to leave my own damn house." "Hell they won't even let me come stay with them." "They say I drink too much." And they don't want that around their children." "Hell they are telling me I can't be around to see my own grandkids." I was sitting on the first step going up the stairs in the house. I'm praying to God quietly in my head. Please don't let Gramps say he can stay here. Lord please, please send him on his way.

Well I couldn't believe my ears. Gramps jumps" up Uncle Sam Jumps up. Gramps grabs Uncle Sam and gives him a great big bear hug and say, "Man you know I can't let stay in the street and sleep in your car," "of course you can stay here."

Uncle Sam turns Gramps around so he can face me. He then looks at me. Our eyes lock on to each other and he gives me that sick evil wink. "How afraid do you think I am right now"? "You damn straight." "Very afraid." "NOW I'M SCREAMING IN MY HEAD SO LOUD! I gave myself a headache. For real I seriously gave myself a headache. I had to go lay down and sleep it off.

So I run upstairs, go to my room and barricade the door. Just as I finished barricading my room, Gramps came to check on me. Here he come tapping on the door. Believe me, I'm mad as hell at Gramps right now. I didn't understand then, all I felt from Gramps at that time was betrayal. Not realizing he really didn't know what his friend was really like.

So Gramps is tapping on the door. "Hattie Mae are you ok? Now as he is asking me, am I ok, he proceeds to push the door open. I jumped up. I'm like (in my head) "Oh My God" my barricade what happened? Gramps came in as if I had nothing at the door. Have you ever in your life felt defenseless? Well magnify that by a hundred. Gramps said, "Girl what's going on in here"? Clean up this mess. I started stuttering. But Gramps you don't understand. He said: HATTIE MAE!! CLEAN IT UP!! CLEAN IT UP NOW! In his low but stern voice.

Oh Boy! So I'm cleaning and crying. Crying because I'm afraid. Of what may happen to me when I'm asleep at night. I have to tell my Grandfather what's going on. "But how"? I'm afraid of telling on Uncle Sam. He once told me if I said anything he was going to kill my dog Frankie. Oh I didn't tell you but I had a puppy at the time, a Shepard. He was only three months old. Uncle Sam kicked him clear across the room one day. Just to make himself clear if I were to talk.

This same Sunday. After I cleaned my room. I went downstairs to get some soda pop and my snacks. As I was walking by Uncle Sam slapped me on my butt. I screamed and ran to Gramps telling him Uncle Sam Slapped me on my butt and it hurt.

He quickly turned to Sam. "Hey man" "Why did you slap Hattie Mae on the butt?" "Come on James you know me better than that." "It was just an innocent tap". "She's over reacting." "That's all, she's just a kid." "You know I wouldn't do anything too harm Hattie Mae." "We are family man" Gramps said ok Sam your right." But don't you ever put your hands on her again. Sam said: you got it Brother, "I'm sorry."

Hattie Mae! "Go upstairs." I will call you when everybody goes home, and when it's time for dinner.

I was to through. I didn't like the outcome of that situation. I was expecting him to get put out, and Gramps not being his friend anymore. Right now I'm so sad, so afraid. All I did was pray.

Because that is what we were taught to do when things went wrong, and you found yourself helpless, with no one to turn to. You turn to God. When you had no one to talk to, you talk to God. When there is no one to protect you, you turn to God for protection. I went upstairs crying with a broken spirit. I went into my Grandfather's room to use the phone. There were two phones in the house one in the kitchen and one in Gramps room. I just had to call home and speak to my Grandmother.

I didn't get an answer the first two times I called, I called the third time all I got was a busy line. I found it to be strange the phone rang two times, and no one answered. I called right back the fourth time, and again I got a busy signal. My Grand Mother was always in the house after church. And for the phone to have rung twice then it went busy that's strange. There are six people living in the home and only one bathroom, so I know everyone wasn't in the bathroom at the same time.

Grand Ma would always cook a great big pot of chicken stew with lots of vegetables and potatoes, her homemade corn bread was from out of this world. "Yummy, Yummy" and a big pot of white rice. My Grandmother fed all those that were hungry in the neighborhood every Sunday. Momma had a big heart.

Right at that moment my heart was feeling sick, I could feel something was wrong. I left my Grandfathers bedroom and sat on the top step. And just as I sat down to call Gramps, the phone rang, and my heart started pounding really fast. He picked up the phone in the kitchen all I could hear him say was. Okay, Yes I hear you. Okay, thank you. And he hung up the phone.

The Taste of Hate

It was still early in the day somewhere around three o'clock. I could hear Gramps whisper to everyone, "Hey I'm sorry it won't be game night tonight." We have a family emergency, the boys all shouted out at the same time. "James what's going on?" We are here to help and support you. "We are brothers". "What's going on man"?

It got real quiet, they were just waiting for Gramps to speak. He broke out in a very quiet cry. Meaning he only had tears falling from his eyes. He replied, it's my daughter. "Oh My God" I sat on the steps shaken and frighten I thought to myself, "oh no, my mommy is dead."

I ran down the stairs screaming and crying. I ran into my Gramps arms and he held me so tight, I lost all blood circulation and oxygen, to my brain and body. "Really." He was squeezing me so tight I felt like I was going to pass out. I was weaving and waving my arms in the air. Trying to breathe gasping for air, the boys was telling him to let me go, they finally pulled me away. When Gramps decided to let me loose from his arms I hit the floor like a ton of bricks.

As I laid on the floor trying to catch my breath. I cried out "GRAMPS! WHAT HAPPENED TO MY MOMMY! No matter what the circumstance is in his life Gramps is always cool calm and collected. He picked me up off the floor and said nothing is wrong with your mommy. It's your Aunt Mary. I then calmed down and went into shock, because, Aunt Mary was invincible to me. Nothing could ever happen to my Aunt Mary.

My world came crashing down. My Aunt Mary suffered a stroke. On her way to the hospital she went into cardiac arrest. She was only nineteen. Aunt Mary lived on the wild side of life. Parties, drugs and alcohol. She graduated top three in her class.

My Aunt Mary was my best friend, my baby sitter and my teacher. Aunt Mary took good care of me. My mother worked two jobs. Aunt Mary was so smart she was downright stupid. I know there is someone in your world just like her. Aunt Mary was more my older sister than my Aunt. My Aunt Mary was never the same after her stroke. It was now my turn to take care of her. She lived three more years after her Stroke." Wait" Sorry, I'm crying right now. I miss her so much.

CHAPTER 6

ANGRY

Everyone is leaving gramps house except for Uncle Sam, because he is now staying with us. I can't wait for this summer to end. I really need to get away from this man.

So we sit down to eat, Gramps and I don't have much of an appetite. So Gramps excuses himself from the table and goes into the living room. I get up, and I began to clean off the table. So I'm still crying while putting the dishes in the sink, and I put the food away in the refrigerator.

Uncle Sam came into the kitchen unable to stand because he was drinking. He grabs the crouch of his pants. And he begins to massage it, and as he is massaging his crouch with one hand, he has his pointer finger of the other hand in the come here motion.

I ran as fast as I could into the living room where Gramps was making music. He stops playing his instruments. He sees me coming full speed ahead. Hey!! Hey!! Hey!! "What's the hurry?' "What's going on"? I sat next to him in silence, afraid to say anything. So I replied; nothing Gramps I'm just sad about Aunt Mary having a stroke. I'm about to take out the garbage.

The Taste of Hate

Uncle Sam heard me say I was taking out the garbage. and somehow he found his way to the back yard. Now before you get to the yard when you walk out the back door in the kitchen, you step into a small room that was added to the house. In this room is a smaller kitchen made only for backyard cook outs. Now Uncle Sam is standing in the yard, not far from the door. I stop to focus, and to take a good look at Uncle Sam. I needed to see what he was up to before I got close to him. Tomorrow is trash pickup day, and I need to take the trash out past the gate.

As I am walking slowly towards Uncle Sam I see him with his dead penis in his hand, shaking it at me. I run back into the big kitchen and I don't see Gramps. I start running and screaming into the living room, I was screaming at the top of my lungs. At this time Gramps walks me back into the kitchen. Uncle Sam put his penis back in his pants. He then runs further out into the backyard and lights his cigar. With the body language, that says: "What"? I'm chilling. Then he says. "Hey brother everything alright"?

I just kept on crying, I can't say a word, just crying. So I continue to take out the trash while Gramps is standing in the door way. Uncle Sam is still smoking his cigar. Gramps waited for me to get back in the house. He turns to me and say; I'm going up stairs and I'm going to bed.

I got stuck in my tracts. I found myself once again unable to move my feet. Although it was a different feeling or I would like to say, a different kind of energy. I felt a more devil like energy. I waited for the sound of Gramps foots steps above my head. I went out into the yard with Uncle Sam, but not to close. You see under the deck there is a water hose for hot and cold water. My initial though was to turn on the hot water and burn the crap out of him. That thought gave me a nice warm fuzzy feeling. Only I couldn't move my feet in his direction it was as if something or someone was holding me down. Every time I tried to move toward him or the water hose I felt this incredible energy holding me in place as if I was drying out in a cement block. Now every time I moved my other foot toward the inside of the house, no problem. So I took that as a sign of God trying to tell me to get my little ass in the house and upstairs.

I took a deep breath and hauled ass up the stairs. Screaming my little head off waving my arms in the air like dragons were after me. "GRAMPS! "GRAMPS! I was so out of breath. When I tell you the stairs looked like the side of a mountain. It seemed like I was never ever going to make it to the top of the stairs.

Gramps was like, "hush up." His face was all wrinkled up like he was trying to be mad at me. He said to me: "Be quiet before the neighbors think I'm doing something to hurt you." I'm in my head like. "Ok Gramps." "I got my own problems. I am not caring about the neighbors right now."

So one-night Uncle Sam begins to test his plan of action. As usual my Gramps was drinking and he was a little sluggish. Every night Uncle Sam had a plan to stay the night with us. Only now he didn't need a plan because he was now living with us.

Uncle Shit Face was trying to figure out a way to move his stank ass upstairs to the spare bedroom. You see Gramps had him sleeping in the basement bedroom. There were nights I didn't sleep or didn't sleep well.

To give you the layout of the second floor. As you approach the top step, the door directly in front of you, slightly to the right was the guest room. Now that you're standing in front of the guest room, about face as if you are going to walk down the hall, stand still now to your left is my room the door next to mine is the bathroom, straight ahead directly across from the guest room is Gramps room.

The Taste of Hate

My bedroom was the creepiest room ever. The house was built from the ground up by my great Aunt, yes that's right my Gramps sister. She died in that house. Now in my room right in front of the closet door, in the ceiling is the entrance to the attic. So every night I heard all kind of weird noises. My imagination was crazy. I didn't know what sound was real or what sound was my imagination. I was just scared.

For instance, a simple knock on the door. First thing popped into my little head was it's the buggy man, or my Aunts ghost, not knowing that the now banging and screaming on the other side of door was Anna. That girl can scream, that's all she did "scream, scream, and scream." That's how she earned the nick name screaming MEEMEE.

Anna is my cousin. Her parents had an emergency and ask Gramps could she come stay the week with me. Her parents had to leave town.

So now it's bed time. We are in bed and my bedroom door is closed. I hear the steps squeaking and making crunching sounds as Uncle Sam tries to creep up the stairs without being heard by my Gramps. I hear the guest bedroom door open, okay now I'm really scared. Not only was I afraid for me, now I have to be afraid and protect my six-year-old cousin. "Shit," how am I going to do that? "Hell I can't protect myself."

Okay I hear the guest room door close. My bed is in a direct line up with the door. It's a small room. So I look at the bottom of the door and I can see Uncle Sam's shadow. I slowly pull the covers over my head and as I take a deep breath, Uncle Sam opens my bedroom door. Now I'm lying there scared to death holding my breath and praying to God to not let me breathe and at the same time, my Gramps opens his bed room door. "Oh boy what a sigh of relief that was." I took a deep breath.

The Taste of Hate

I heard my Gramps say, "Hay man what the hell are you doing in the kid's room"? Uncle Sam was lost for words, but only for a very short moment. My Gramps said again. "What the hell are you doing in my granddaughter's room"? I was like, "yeah gramps, get him." Meanwhile I'm still hiding under the covers. So Uncle Sam responded; Oh! Oh! Brother I'm sorry I left my glasses down stairs, I thought this was the bathroom. So Gramps told him, next time use the bathroom down stairs in the basement.

Now gramps is checking up on us, as soon as he opened the door, Anna in her little sweet crackly voice said to Gramps "I'm scared." "I want to go home," can I go now please? She made me cry. I was afraid as well. Not only for me but for her.

I cried on and off throughout the night. The less I cried the angrier I became. Angry because of the fear Uncle Sam put in me and my little cousin. It was my job to protect her. Uncle Sam made me feel like I was about to fail at doing so. I became more and more angry.

I'm a Brooklyn night, we kick ass and be afraid later. Now you know as well as I do. At eight I'm not kicking anyone's ass. I then became worried at the punishment I would get from my mother and my uncle for not taking care of, and protecting Anna. I had to protect Anna and myself. Geez!! Talk about pressure. How in the hell was I going to do this? Wow I forgot all about my fear.

I had fear of not knowing what Uncle Sam had planned. That was making me angry. It was not a good feeling. My stomach felt like a bottomless pit. I could feel my spit free falling in my stomach and it never landed. Not fully understanding what my feeling was, I knew it was bad. My gut just didn't sit well when Uncle Sam was around.

All of a sudden I started thinking. And that just made me more nervous and even more uncomfortable. I started to connect the dots. I started thinking about Uncle Shit face in the yard and shaking he's limp dead penis at me and telling me to come closer.

The only thing I knew about penises, is boys have them and they were for peeing and making mud. "Ewe" the things we played in as kids back in the day. "Yeah I know I'm shaking my head to." Laughing out loud!

The look in Uncle Sam's eyes changed. The tone in his voice just wasn't the same anymore. The way he called my name was like, he was getting up the nerve to do something he knew wasn't right. Sometimes Uncle Sam would call my name and it was as though my name got caught up in his throat. And he sometimes he had a hard time spitting it out. He would begin to say my name and half way through it, he would stop. Hey Hat, or it was almost like someone or something grabbed him by the throat. Hey I'm eight and my cousin Anna is just six years old. We needed a bus ticket quick fast and in a hurry.

I was becoming more and more, angry and my love for Uncle Sam was turning into hate. He had this new thing when he was in the house. Whenever my Grandfather would leave the room Uncle Sam would pull out a hand full of candy, and he would tell Anna to come and get some. Hell, what did she know about the candy trick, she's six and like candy. What kid doesn't?

Now if she was from Brooklyn and not a sheltered child. She would have told Uncle Sam no. And maybe she would have told him to go shove it.

She had a little fear of him because of what happened the night before. When he was trying to sneak into our bedroom. Six year olds tend to forget about being frighten, for a moment when one is holding a hand full of candy. After all, no real harm was done. So

The Taste of Hate

Anna falls for the, come and get the candy trick. Next thing I know she's sitting on his lap.

Now Gramps is in the basement kitchen where the booze and beer is kept. It is also where all the fried foods are made. It was fish night.

Ok let's take a quick tour of the basement. At the foot of the stairs straight ahead is a living room, under the stairs is the boiler and right next to that is the laundry area.

Some of you might know what I'm talking about. When it came to the washing machine you were the rinse cycle. Do you remember the washing machine with no lid and two rolling pins? You had to push the clothes through to get the water out, and in the process you got your fingers caught in it, Ouch!!

The next room which also has a door leading to the back yard was the kitchen. That's where Grandpa was frying fish and getting a few cans of beer. I don't want to confuse you we had three kitchens. One on the main floor. Now the main kitchen has a back door. Right pass that back door take one step down a really small kitchen was built. It only had a stove and a small sink. This was the kitchen used for backyard cook outs. Down stairs in the basement was the third kitchen. The basement was set up like a small apartment. Just keep in mind anything being cooked with more than a cup of cooking oil was not done in the main kitchen.

So now let's go back upstairs. I'm sitting across from Uncle Sam about to shit on myself, because Anna is still sitting on Uncle Sam's lap. I don't know what to do. The whole time I'm watching Uncle Sam. He's watching me with this really evil look. His face was talking to me with no words. "Yeah go head say something." My skin was crawling with sweat.

The Taste of Hate

There he sat in the arm chair with these light blue panty shorts and a white dress shirt and black saddles. Anna was wearing a really pretty pink polka dot sundress and matching pink panties with pink and white ribbons in her hair. I dressed her like my Auntie would have dressed me. Watching her sit in Uncle Sam's lap made me wish I never dressed her so cute.

I'm sitting on the floor in front of them. Uncle Sam and I are still in starring mode with each other. It's hot as hell today. It is so hot the paint on the porch is peeling. It felt like a hundred degrees outside and one hundred twenty in the house. All we have are a bunch of fans circulating hot air. Uncle Sam starts to rub Anna's leg. At this time my heart is racing. I'm sweating and I started to breath very heavy. "OH MY GOD" I'm in my head. ("What the fuck am I going to do now?")

Keep in mind I'm from Brooklyn and I come from a cussing family. Everything is Fuck this and mother fuck that. Just then the doorbell rang, I snatched Anna and ran down the stairs with Gramps. It was the police looking for Uncle Sam. His wife Delores reported the car stolen. She told the cops she spotted the car at my Grandfathers house. What a blessing that was. After all the commotion, Uncle Sam was gone for five days. This is going to be a long summer.

So now it's Sunday and we start all over again. We go to church, we go to the bootlegers, we go home, Grandpa sets up and the friends come by, Gramps crew. Only this time Uncle Sam is already drunk or he is putting on a great act. Anna and I are off to bed. To my, not surprise self, Uncle Sam didn't go home. He's still staying with us. Anna's Parents will be picking her up tomorrow which will be Monday. My gut was telling me not to let Anna sleep by herself. I don't like sleeping with anyone, and after spending a few nights in the bed with Anna. I felt she needed her own space so I talked Gramps into letting her go back into the guest bedroom.

So we go to our own room and the noise in the attic was crazy. Now just so you know the Attic is empty. Nothing is in the attic, only dust. Gramps had the attic cleaned and insulated. "So will someone" "PLEASE!! Tell me why it sounds like a tornado in the attic.

I was scared. I ran in Anna's room with the intention of jumping in the bed. I dislike twin beds. Geez! I jump so high and hard, I hit the bed bounced and rolled one time, and hit the floor." OH" I was in so much pain. I couldn't get off the floor. So I told Anna to go in my room and get my pillow and covers. I was going to sleep on the floor. Gramps is down stairs in the basement, I never seen him run or maybe I should say, hop so fast in my life. Gramps got to the guest bedroom in record time. He didn't see me because I was on the floor between the wall and the bed.

CHAPTER 7

MY AUNT SISSY

Anna was coming out of my room with my blankets and pillow. And the doorbell rang. So Gramps turns to go back down stairs. Never seeing me Gramps tells us to; "Go to bed and stop playing around."

Well thank you Jesus it was my great Aunt. My Gramps Sister Aunt Sissy. Anna got in the bed threw me the covers and we just laid there quietly. Anna fell asleep, I might have dosed off here and there. After a while I hear footsteps coming up the stairs. It's Aunt Sissy. She goes into my room and quietly calls out my name. "Hattie Mae," piss, "Hattie." As she gets closer to the bed she realizes I'm not there. So she takes two steps into Anna's room and calls out my name. "Hattie Mae you in here"? I whisper: Yes, Auntie I'm on the floor. Auntie ask: girl! "What are you doing on the floor?" I said in a soft, weak and painful voice. I fell and hurt myself.

So she picks me up and takes me back to my room. I grabbed her so tight. I whispered into Aunties ear. Please don't leave me here by

The Taste of Hate

myself. Please stay, go home tomorrow. PLEASE! PLEASE! PLEASE! I broke down crying and shaking like a leaf. I told her all of what was going on with Uncle Sam. Auntie had blood in her eyes. She said, I will take care of Sam.

Auntie calmly gets up she goes into the bathroom she gets a paper cup and some BC Powder. She mixes it with a little water and told me to drink it. I didn't want to at first, but I was in so much pain.

My Aunt Sissy was dying of cancer. Aunt Sissy also had high blood pressure and she was a diabetic. Auntie laid in the bed with me and we talked all night. I wanted to ask her questions and I couldn't. Again my words

were stuck in my throat. This time I was not chocking. My Auntie said many things to me that night. All I could do was listen. None of which made any since to me at the time. It definitely became clear to me as I got older.

The one thing that really stuck to me, was her telling me. Always know when God is in your presents, and never leave the presents of God. "Can I please get an Amen"?

I fell asleep in her arms. I didn't realize at the time Aunt Sissy was giving me a life lesson, and all that wisdom, was from her own life experience. "I was in school that night."

The morning came, I was facing the window and it was the most beautiful day I had ever seen. The sun was brighter than ever. The sky was clear blue and two white doves where sitting on my window ledge looking at me. My Auntie had her Arms wrapped around me. Oh my what a good comfy feeling. It was truly a God given day. I just laid there and relished in the moment. And as I took a deep breath to suck it all in. My Auntie was taking her last breath. I felt a chill run threw my body. And here we go again I froze. Except this time, I felt safe. It felt strange but safe, and peaceful.

The Taste of Hate

The doves are still sitting there, and with a blink of an eye they disappeared into the air and at that moment my aunts arm around me became a little heavy, I couldn't move.

I began to panic. It's like I knew but I didn't know. I had to once again process what was going on. "MAN! OH!! MAN" once I did process what happened I screamed!! Well let me tell you like this. "I screamed so damn loud the neighbors were knocking on the door." True talk. For real the block was in their nighties at the front door at six am in the morning.

Gramps came running in the room. He said In his quiet voice: "what the hell are you" -----he paused. Them he started crying Oh God!! OH

God NO! NO! NO! He Screamed "SISSY" Wake up, NO! "Sissy not now". "Lord OH God." For the first and time in my life I heard my Grandfather cry. He came closer to the bed and started shaking Aunt Sissy, telling her. "Sissy wake up." "Come on, please God wake her up" "just one more day." I'm like in my head in a quiet voice. HEY! Gramps Aunt Sissy isn't getting up. So could you please, just stop trying to wake her up, and get her off me? Now I'm in my head screaming. But for real, all I could do was lay there and cry.

By this time some of the neighbors came in through the back door. The back door was often left unlocked. Back then you could do things like leave your door open, and sleep in peace without anyone trying come in your house.

I now hear a thunder of foots steps running up the stairs. Yay! Neighbors to the rescue. By now Anna is up, she ran in the room before the crowd and stood by the window. I was almost losing her in the ray of sun light blinding me. The sun was out and doing its thing. As I got older and looking back on that particular moment in time. I now believe that strange but calming ray of light was Aunt Sissy. By now everyone is talking at the same time, lots and lots of commotion I heard someone say, move the baby. Someone else said; what? "I said move the baby." In case you didn't know, that was me they were talking about. Finally, they pulled me out of Aunt Sissy's arm. She had me in a choke hold. It was ok when she was breathing.

Someone must have called nine one, one. Because the next thing you know, there where cops all over the place. Talking about things getting out of control. Oh My God!! It got crazy. They had gramps in hand cuffs. They grabbed me and Anna and took us down stairs. They put the neighbors on the porch and in the dining room. My Gramps was in the back seat of the police car.

Anna and I were in the living room. We heard the cop say call social service. That punk ass Uncle Sam snuck out the house through the back. I saw it with my own eyes.

I knew social service wasn't a good call, hell I'm from Brooklyn. Social service only meant.

They come, kids get taken from their parents and put in foster care, or they checking to see if a man is living with your momma. They be all in your closet checking shoes counting tooth brushes. Some of you know what I'm talking about. It was a scary moment. Now I hear one cop say. We have the murder suspect in custody. Familiar words when you're from Brooklyn. I just knew in my heart that if we left the house we would be in deep, deep shit.

Miss Ray from right next door to Gramps house sat beside me. She gave me a great big hug and said. Baby what happened? I said sobbing crying and whimpering all at the same time with one word coming out between each sob and whimper, and in haling or should I say snorting up falling snot from my nose. I replied, Sheeree -jaja- ust died. She she - wa- wa was just slee- ping. Miss Ray stood up and in a very loud voice. She just took over. Miss Ray screamed out "EVERYBODY GET THE HELL UP OUT OF HEAR", "RIGHT NOW EXCEPT FOR THE POLICE". OUT! EVERYBODY, NOW. If

The Taste of Hate

"YOU DON'T LIVE HEAR GET OUT NOW AND GO HOME".

Miss Ray put so much fear in everyone, they were running through the doors front and back like roaches in a burning building. One police officer reached to grab Miss Ray by her arm and she gave him such an evil eye he just backed up. He was very young and very new on the job as a cop. Miss Ray told the cop in charge. Sissy died in her sleep.

When they got the call some ass hole told them they heard screaming and they think someone was killed. Shaking my head. "Damn Dummies," I was the one screaming, that was after I realized Auntie died.

Now two social service workers were walking in the house so Anna and I ran and hid behind Miss Ray. Next my real Uncle Mike walks in with Uncle Shit Face. For once Uncle Sam did something right. I was a little pissed off at him for abandoning us. But unexpectedly he pulled through and did the right thing for Gramps.

Uncle Mike pulled one of the officers with a lot of stripes on his shirt to the side. They were in the corner talking to each other. Meanwhile the two Social workers are trying to ask us questions and Miss Ray told us not to say a word.

The social worker was whispering a threat in my ear. She said she was going to cut my hair off if I didn't run outside. Again I'm from Brooklyn NY. I was told by my Uncle. Black people should never run unless they are in the Olympics.

Here comes Anna always on point with her crying. Anna cried and screamed so hard and loud The Social Workers ran outside. They couldn't bare the screeching sounds Anna made.

The Taste of Hate

Now that the police officer and Uncle Mike were finished talking. The police officer told the social workers they can leave. Because Uncle Mike was the next of kin. So they left, and the next thing I know Gramps is walking back into the house without the hand cuffs. Until this day I don't think I have ever cried so long and hard in my life.

Gramps called Aunt Sissy's Dr. and the cops stood around and sat until her Doctor showed up. In the meantime, Miss Ray went into the kitchen and made breakfast coffee and tea for everyone left in the house.

Anna and I go upstairs to put on some clothes. I was afraid of going into my room because Aunt Sissy's dead body is in my bed. Anna still not too sure what's going on. She asks me was I going to wake Aunt Sissy up, I

said no shaking my head. So I creep in my room to get my clothes. I grab my clothes and I ran out as fast as I could.

As I'm running out of the room Uncle Sam is standing there and he scoops me up in the air. He holds me tight to his body. I'm fighting to get away, and at the same time he is feeling and touching me, all over my body, my butt and my private parts. I'm crying quietly fighting and punching him as hard as I can, to get away. Then I notice The Gold chain on his neck belong to Aunt Sissy. Now I found my voice. "Do you know that bastard robbed my dead Auntie?"

I started screaming again. This time I screamed out loud, but only for a split second, and that was ok. Because it was long enough for someone to hear me. Suddenly my ears went deaf. My voice was silent once again. My body went numb to anything touching me. Once again I hear my heart beating, my heart is beating faster than a horse in a race. I can still see myself struggling to get away from Uncle Sam.

Out of nowhere I see my Auntie Sissy standing there behind Uncle Sam, with her arms extended out as if she is reaching for me. I stopped fighting to get out of Uncle Sam's arms, and reached out to grab Auntie Sissy. As I reached for Auntie, I landed on my feet, Uncle Sam was rolling down the stairs.

I sat on the very top of the steps and watched Uncle Sam as he hit the bottom. He looked up at me as if I was the cause of him falling. Uncle Mike watched quietly as Uncle Sam landed at his feet. This fool told the cops I pushed him down the stairs. Do you remember how I told you how bad he smelled, well he had so much alcohol in him he just smelled drunk. All I could say was good for you Uncle Shit Face. He broke his arm and fractured his hip. My question was. Where was the cop watching the room?

Thank You Auntie Sissy. I knew it was her doing. I learned then spirits are not only real but they can be good. I was no longer afraid of the noise in the attic. Nor was I ever afraid of creepy things. Well some creepy things.

Uncle Shit Face was creepy. Yes, I was still afraid of him.

The Doctor finally arrived. He spoke to the police officer in charge. He told them how sick Auntie was and it was just a matter of time before she would die, and there was no need for an autopsy. He said she can go straight to the funeral home. So now my room is off limits even to me. I was told by Gramps not to go back into my room. Believe me I had no problem with that. I wasn't afraid, I was just curious.

The only social media we had back in the day was the house phone pay phone and word of mouth. Oh! I Forgot Telegrams was very popular back then, and I am here to tell you. I believe it worked just the same. Because shortly after lunch, we had family from six states in the house. Family had already communicated with each other on who had to be picked up from the airport and who had to be picked up from Greyhound. Everybody was there mommy, daddy, Aunties. Uncles.

The Taste of Hate

Cousins and friends. People were laughing and crying, crying and laughing. It just seemed to me, to be one big party.

Gramps was playing his instruments, church songs was sung, and food was pouring in from the neighbors like crazy, and yes I pigged out. Sorry my belly is full now and I'm feeling pretty lonely. Even though the house was full of kids my age, and lots of family members. I just felt lost.

So I went upstairs and sat in the hall with my back up against the wall between my room and the bathroom.   I was afraid to go in the room and take one last peek at Aunt Sissy. I heard talking and laughter and people walking around in the room. I thought my mother and a few others were in the room with my dead Aunt Sissy. I sat there for a long time. Then finally my mother came upstairs I jumped up and ran into her arms. I really thought she was in the room with Auntie. So I asked her,

"Mommy who's in the room with Auntie"? She said, I don't know let's see.

Well with me still in her arms, she shifted me to her hip side and opened the door. No one was in the room except Aunt Sissy. Auntie looked so peaceful.

Uncle Mike is yelling throw the house. Ok everybody Uncle is here. Uncle was another one of my real Uncles, and Uncle was his first name. My favorite game with him was, what your name is. He would say Uncle and I would say, uncle who? What's your name? Uncle what? John, Jerry, Mike, what is your first Name? Please use your imagination on this one. Go ahead take a moment. So he was every ones Uncle per say. Laughing out loud that's funny to me. Anyway Uncle was a preacher. As soon as he came in everyone gathered as he began to preach a prayer. Hallelujah, HALLELUJAH! Amen!!

The Taste of Hate

Then as he walked up the stairs to where Auntie Sissy was. Everyone got in line along the stairway, family first then friends as Uncle prayed for Aunties soul. Those who wanted to see her and pray with Uncle did so until the funeral home came to pick her body up.

Now a couple of days go by. We are at church having our home going service for Aunt Sissy. It was a full house. People standing in the back, people sitting in the aisle.

There is nothing like a home going service at a black Southern Baptist Church. "Man oh Man" we partied like rock stars. There's no Party like a church Party. I should say a going home service. Everybody singing and clapping, dancing and praising the lord.

Friends and family were paying tribute to Aunt Sissy she was a magnificent woman. Not a dry eye in the house.

In come Uncle Shit Face. Late, but he showed up. With his broke arm in a sling and being pushed in a wheel chair due to a fractured hip. I was hoping he had broken it all the way. You know, like you would snap a wish bone in half. A man like him don't deserve to walk.

I was sitting there laughing my ass off. Seeing him in pain was like sweet sugar running like a rapid river threw my veins. Besides who told the jerk he was family. Do you know that ass rolled up to the front and tried to squeeze his stinky broke ass in the seat? I wished they had dropped his ass when they took him out of the wheel chair. "Fake crying, looking like a jackass." "I HATE HIM!

Everyone in God's country knew Aunt Sissy didn't like Uncle Sam. The story told. Aunt Sissy got away with doing some serious jail time for kicking Uncle Shit faces ass. The real Story told was, Aunt Sissy almost killed him. He spent three weeks in ICU. With head injuries, two broken ribs, and she broke his jaw. WOW! This man has had a lot of broken bones in his day. They say Aunt Sissy got locked up for a day because he was drunk

and defenseless. No one ever spoke about why she did it.

The home going service has come to an end. Now we are taking that long never ending and empty feeling ride to the cemetery. My mind was trying to remember everything Aunt Sissy was telling me the night before she died.

We get to the cemetery to say our last good byes. Everyone has their final flower in their hand ready to lay it on Aunt Sissy's casket. "Now picture this in your mind" we are all in a

circle around a big hole in the ground, and the casket setting close to the hole opposite of where I am standing. Uncle Shit face is in the wheel chair. I'm holding his hand only because we are in prayer. Our heads are at the same level because he's sitting in the wheel chair and I am standing next to him. My cousin is holding my other hand.

Now while Uncle is saying the dust to dust prayer. Uncle Shit face is in my ear telling me if I say anything he's going to have my whole family killed. In the meantime, he is massaging the center of my hand. Me not knowing what that was about. I knew it wasn't good. My eye sight was so clouded with tears of fear. I couldn't see where my mother or Grandfather was. I mean I was really blinded by my own tears.

We are standing close to the hole of the grave. Aunt Sissy's coffin was on the opposite side of us. Out of know where the sky turned black. Everyone started running. Uncle Shit Face friends left him, and "BOOM" the rain fell so hard it was bringing people down to their knees.

The Taste of Hate

So now he has no one to push him out of the rain. "Oh My God! I'm laughing my ass off right now." "Ok you have to Jump in my head for this one" Uncle Shit Face can't roll himself out of the mud. "I'm laughing sorry" So he tries to get up, only he's too close to the hole. "SORRY" I'm still laughing. He can't push the wheel chair back. And oops! Man Over Board "BOOM! In he goes. "Sorry, I'm Still laughing". All you hear is a scream, "Lord no not me! "I'm sorry lord". "I'm not ready lord". Somebody please help me!

Now those that are drunk starts running faster, because they don't see Uncle Sam in the hole they just hear a distant voice. Me, well of course I saw him go down. I was probably the only one with eyes on him.

I was so quiet, if I you were in church with me, you could have heard a church mouse piss on carpet. I wasn't telling anyone I saw him fall in the hole. So Of course they realized Uncle Sam fell in the ground. So they hoist Uncle

Shit Face up out of the grave and sent him back to the hospital.

Now that the home going service is over and Auntie Sissy is in the ground. The next day, everyone is packing up to go home.

All of a sudden Anna runs a high fever and breaks out in these little prickly bumps. And she's scratching like she has flees. Lucky her she got the measles. I already had them. The fever came from an ear infection she developed from the rain. She really got soaked. Lucky her she got to go home. Lucky me, I got to stay another two long weeks. I was relieved Anna was going home, now all I had to worry about was me.

I promise you I'm not going to let you read about another rape case. I refuse to live my life as a victim. I want you to understand what I'm about to tell you, and to the best of my ability, I will describe to you my hate, at its highest level. Please don't get this emotion of hate confused with rage.

My parents went home. The plan was for Gramps to take me home two days before school starts. Uncle Shit Face returned after a couple of days. He just stopped by to say hello. It had appeared he didn't suffer any more injuries than he already had, just some scrapes and bruises.

My vacation was almost over. Two weeks to go. As I awake each morning to greet the sun, "ugh" is the first sound I make, and I close the curtains as tight as they can get. At this time, I'm still at my grandfather's house. It's been a few days since Aunt Sissy's going home service.

CHAPTER 8

THE SEDUCTION

Gramps always kept his curtains closed whether he had a card game or shooting cramps. I didn't matter, he didn't like the knowing people were looking into his house. He would turn the lights on, and I would walk behind him turning the lights off. It was me unknowingly slipping into the darkness. I began to hate the sight of light.

It's Sunday again. Uncle Shit face aka you know who, Uncle Sam. Came by as scheduled after church. This time Uncle Shit Face, was the first one to arrive. I ran to the door to open it. Screaming out loud. I GOT IT GRAMPS!!! I GOT IT. I ran to the door with a butcher knife in my hand. See I was in the kitchen looking for something to protect myself with.

I opened the door, Sam went to reach for the top of my head as to pet me like a puppy or something. Well my hands went straight up in the air, Yeah!! "That's right" with the knife in my hand. nice and sharp. Well my hand went up and he's went down. All I heard Sam say, was "ouch oh shit". You cut me! At first, my instinct was to make an apology. I paused, I just looked him in his eyes and walked back into the kitchen. Yes!! I felt a little victory, and I'm here to tell you it felt really good. I wanted more. I wanted him to feel pain all day every day.

Shortly after his wife Delores showed up, as she does every Sunday. This Sunday seem to be a bit different. Delores seemed to be calmer. Uncle Shit Face reached into his pocket, and gave Delores what was in it.

Well the unspeakable happened that night. My Grandfather got really sick. And he had to be taken to the hospital. I wanted to call my mother and Sam wasn't having it.

What I didn't know was my Grandfather was trying to stop drinking and was having really bad withdrawals. He had to be hospitalize. So they took him to the VA hospital to detox.

Well here I am left all alone with Sam. He turns to me and in a soft quiet voice. Hey kid, I'm not going to bother you. I just want your Gramps to get better he's like my brother. And I promise you I will take good care of you. Boy was I a sucker. He offered me a soda pop. Of course I'm going to say yes. "Remember I'm a Kid", never knew he was going to lace my soda pop with his pain pills.

"OH MY GOD" I was out like a light. When I woke up I found myself in the basement of my grandfather's house. I knew I was in the basement because it always smelled like mildew.

I was dandling from the ceiling butt ass naked. If you can imagine what I was feeling at that moment. Things were still a little foggy. I was trying to pull myself together. I tried to scream for help only to realize my mouth was gagged and taped.

The Taste of Hate

At that same moment, due to the fact I was hungry I smelled chocolate. I thought it was my imagination. Now I'm confused, "why do I smell chocolate in the basement, of all places?" I don't know if its day or night. I didn't feel the rag tied around my head which covered my eyes. I was blind folded. And I realized the chocolate I was smelling was all over my body. Can you believe this man covered me in liquid chocolate? I was just dangling in the air covered in my favorite Bosco mix.

Lord help me, any other time I would have thought I had died and went to heaven, with all that chocolate over me. Instead I was in hell and alive.

I could hear more than one set of foots steps above my head. No voices. The extra set of footsteps were leading out the front door. As I hear the footsteps of Sam coming down the stairs. I began to shiver, then a hard trimmer. I felt like I was convulsing.

If you noticed, I no longer call Sam Uncle. No Uncle would ever do what he has done to me or anyone that was family. So after what appeared to be several minutes, I could hear absolutely nothing. Boy was I exhausted. I believe I went back to sleep. Because there was a time laps where I couldn't remember anything. Remember I was drugged with Sam's pain medication. My nervous system went into warp drive. So of course I went back to sleep." I was high as hell.

I woke up feeling hot liquid running down my legs and between my thighs. Well sorry folks it's not what you think. "I was pissing on myself" I mean It was a never ending flow of piss. I must have pissed for a full minute, well it felt like it. I'm sure you took a piss, and sat there saying to yourself. "Damn that's a lot of water."

I can hear Sam's foots steps coming down the stairs. "Oh My God" I smell food. I got so excited I started farting." Oh Boy" what a stinky situation. I just wanted to eat. Then I thought about the way he slipped me his pain medication. I suddenly lost my appetite. I got nervous all over again. Then on top of that I realized Sam was looking at my naked body. I started shaking and got the trimmers all over again. This whole time Sam never – said - a - word. "I mean not one word," Since he hung me in the basement. And you know me, I was too afraid to say anything. I could feel him under me cleaning up my urine. Boy was I scared shitless.

Sam took me down. I'm still tied, gagged and blind folded. He carried me to the laundry room and hosed me down. Now I'm shivering from the air blowing against my wet body.

Sam then carries me back into the room. He hung me back in place, as if I was a piece of pork waiting to be smoked. My hunger pains are getting stronger.

Sam begins to smear liquid chocolate around my neck. He smeared some on my lips, and that's when I confirmed Sam was using BOSCO chocolate syrup on my body. He's just pouring, and pouring, the chocolate down my frail body. I can feel it roll off my shoulders and slowly sliding down my arms and dripping off my fingertips. I can feel it rolling down my back and in between my butt cheeks, down the back of my thighs before I knew it, my body was fully covered in sweet chocolate. I was so hungry I tried to lick myself.

Still no sound from Sam. Next thing I know; I was feeling his hot breath in my ear. I can't quite understand what he is saying. And I didn't want to know. Next I feel these long slow licks from the tip of my tail bone up the center of my back to the center of my neck. He is holding me in place as he stands behind me with his left arm around my waist with his middle finger pressing against my belly button for support. He is using his right hand to massage my body and spread chocolate syrup. As he slowly spreads his right hand down the side of my frail little body and he gets to my feet, he begins to lotion it with the chocolate syrup in between my toes and the bottom of my feet. Then he slowly glides his hand up the back of my leg and in a circle motion around my butt cheeks.

At this time every muscle in my body is locked. My butt cheeks were so tight a fly couldn't crawl in it. Sam was really getting angry. I refused to unlock my body. After all it was my only defense.

He kept rubbing and sliding he's hand up and down, and at times pressing really hard to get in-between my butt cheeks.

He got so frustrated he ties my already tied feet with even more rope. He unhooks me from the ceiling and places me on the sofa which was covered in what I called the guest sheets. They were the old sheets in the house that didn't match but were clean enough for overnight guest.

Sam then pins me down with his body. All he has on at this time is a pair of shorts. As I lay there pinned down to the sofa he has me on my side with my knees in my chest. I go numb praying he don't kill me. Praying someone will come to my rescue, praying God will come and kill him. Praying anyone would come and kill him.

Sam is now licking me like I'm an Ice pop in the sun and he's thirsty. He is licking me rapidly like a crazy man. The more I shiver the faster he licks. So I began to calm down at this point I could feel his finger sliding back and forth in my butt hole I panicked, and locked them butt cheeks once again only this time it really hurts, Sam was trying to pull his finger out of my butt. So I relaxed long enough for him to pull his finger out. Then I went back to butt cheek lock down mode.

He then took the blind folds off my eyes. He still had me gagged and tied. He sat there looking into my eyes. All I could do was stare back and cry. I was afraid to take my eyes off him. I needed to keep my eyes on him to see what was coming next.

The longer I looked at Sam the more I felt hatred, I felt anger. In my head I said: "how dare you do this to me." "What did I do to deserve this? The Sam I knew growing up was no longer the man I knew this summer. My Uncle Sam would take us to the park by ice cream cotton candy jelly beans and soda pop. Uncle Sam was a fun loving drunk. I have no idea who this man is.

Sam was trying to lick me clean of all the chocolate he had smeared over my body. At this point he had his head between my legs pressing down my inner thighs to the sofa. I was desperately trying to close my legs. He as licking and sucking on my vagina. There I go again my body started the termers again.

I soon realized again my tremors was a turn on for him. I got him excited. It took a minute but I was finally able to relax myself, as I was relaxing I started to think clear.

The only thing I could come up with at the time was to fart in his face. Well I tried so hard to fart it just wasn't happening. I would not give up because again, it was the only defense I could come up with. So I stopped trying only because I was hurting myself.

Lucky me I had to pee and take a shit. So naturally I tried to hold it, then I thought to myself what would happened if I just went to the bathroom on his face. Well I'm here to tell you I did the unthinkable. I let loose everything.

Finally, Sam speaks. "Oh! "What the fuck" "you little mother fucker"! "Yuck". Sam Gets up and runs into the basement bathroom. He's in there for a while.

The Taste of Hate

I just laid there I was unable to free myself from the ropes. I had nothing but prayer. The more I prayed the less it was helping me feel better. My heart and soul began to fill its self with anger and rage. My prayers were getting short and I started praying a little slower. My words became fewer and far in between.

Finally, I heard the water turn off in the bathroom. I had nothing, no plan no way out, nothing. All I had was my new found anger and hatred I now have for Sam.

He now enters the basement living room where he left me laying in my own fesses and urine. He untied my feet not once did he look me straight in the face. Not once did he even try to look into my eyes. I just kept staring at him wishing my eyes had daggers, and they would somehow magically shoot from my eyes into his and just blow him up into tiny little pieces.

Once he untied my feet Sam grabbed the rope that had my hands tied. He got me to my feet and took me in to the laundry room where he once again hosed me down. I felt like a wet noodle he just wouldn't stop hosing me down it seem like it was taking forever.

I was so tired and worn out, all I wanted to do at this point was to eat and sleep. I knew sleeping wasn't an option. I was starving. I knew not to drink anything because that's how he got me hanging in the basement. That's when he snuck his pain medication in my drink the first time. I didn't want to give him a second chance to drug me.

Now after I'm all hosed down and still hand tied. Sam slowly walks me upstairs to the main floor. All the windows are closed, curtain drawn tight. Seeing how dark it was and the food on the table lead me to believe it was night time. He sat me down to the table butt naked. At this point I didn't care I just wanted to eat.

Sam came back to the table sitting to my right with his plate of food and two glasses of lemonade. I was not about to drink the lemonade. Boy was I thirsty. I took my time eating so I wouldn't choke. Back home you had to eat all your food before you got anything to drink, so I'm good no need to drink the spiked lemonade. Sam Made ham hocks black eyed pea's rice, fried chicken legs, gravy and biscuits. He and Gramps were great cooks. Well I'm eating like it was my last meal. Sam was smarter than an eight-year-old. He didn't spike the lemonade he

spiked the damn beans I felt the room spinning, I couldn't keep my eyes open or hold myself up. "BOOM" I was out again. Shaking my head right now, just as you are. He got me again.

I woke up to loud voices coming from down stairs some of the voices were recognizable, while some of the voices were strange. I take a deep breath trying to focus on where I was, and what was going on. Trying to figure out what was going to be my next move.

Well first I have to tell you as I took a deep breath, I smelled like Jean' Nate' I looked under the covers and found I was fully dressed in my Pajamas. Still drugged and unable to move. I went back to sleep, feeling a little safer, only because I had on clothes and I was in my room with the door closed.

When I woke up I could hear the TV on. It was the news. I could hear the news reporter say it was Tuesday morning. Remember my Grandfather got sick Sunday. I have had more twenty-four hours of pure darkness. I wake up in my room the sunlight is as bright, and as beautiful as always.

A bright ray of sun shine was hitting the winnows. I looked through the window pane. I could see a beautiful white dove just sitting there watching me in silence. The white dove reminded me of the morning My Auntie Sissy died.

There is no way anyone at that time or this time, can convince me that that dove was not my Auntie Sissy. I smiled and prayed to the dove as if it was my Auntie Sissy. "Auntie please help me, please Auntie" "don't fly away please ask God can you stay and help me out" "Please Auntie." For some reason at that moment I realized I lost a little bit of my faith. I felt as If God turned his back on me and he forgot to turn back around. I needed me Auntie to go and talk to him on my behalf.

I started singing in my head HOLD to his hand, God's unchanging hands. So as I lay there singing the last church song I heard before leaving home, the door slowly opens. "Oh man" here we go again. I balled up into a knot, and once again I locked every "muscle" in my body.

To my surprise it was my mother. All I could do was lay there and cry like a five-day long abandon infant. She must have been there for a while. Because as she entered the room, she said: "Hey sleepy head" about time you woke up. I silently cried so hard, I had no fight left in me at that moment.

My mother picked me up and held me tight and for the first time, being in her arms wasn't where I wanted to be. I didn't want anyone to touch me. I felt detached from the world. I gently pushed myself away from my mother's arms. I curled myself into a fetal position not once looking into my mother's eyes.

My mother got up to exit my room, as she was pulling my bedroom door closed my Uncle, named Uncle, was already at the top of the stairs. I heard them talking. Uncle asked my mother, how is Hattie? She replied, not to good. I think she already know. Uncle replied WOW! You think Sam told her. My mother replied I'm not sure, "by the way where is Sam"? Uncle said I don't know.

The Taste of Hate

So now I'm thinking what the hell is going on. I just laid there. Now Uncle came into the room and he ask me, where did Uncle Sam go? Now just so you and I are on the same page. My mother has keys to the house. Sam was gone before my mother and Uncle got there. So when Uncle ask me where did Sam go? I never answered. Then he asked me, who told you Gramps died last night? I could have died and gone straight to hell just then.

Ok so maybe that wasn't my Auntie in the form of a white Dove, and maybe it was my Gramps at the window this morning. My life was just getting darker and darker.

I became Isolated and none communicative. I stopped being the lovely active girl in the world. My world became a struggle between good and evil. God and sometimes Jesus on one hand, and the devil himself on the other. And I'm here to tell you, I got real hard with everyone at times. And it became even harder believing in God.

It's sad to say everyone miss took my behavior and blamed it on the loss of my Auntie Sissy and my Grandfather. Shaking my head once again.

All of what's going on I'm still human and still a kid. I was hungry. I got out of bed and took a bath. I then returned to my room to get dressed for the day. Still no sign of Sam. And I'm sure you know I went searching the house for him. I was afraid to go in the basement by myself. So I went out back and looked through the back door glass. I couldn't see anything.

Uncle was out back parking the car. He got out the car and said come on let's take a peek. I need to bring something's upstairs. I stood at the basement door. Uncle yelled at me. "Hattie" what are you afraid of? I never answered. "Hattie" What's going on? "You seem a bit different". "Like, something is bothering you" I'm here for you if you ever need to talk. Now, I need you to remember that Uncle is a man of God.

The Taste of Hate

As we are walking into the basement I'm hiding behind Uncle. I was walking in his footsteps and as we walked through the basement, it smelled and look squeaky clean. Sam cleaned the basement so well, that old mildew smell was gone.

I looked in the washer machine and nothing. It's empty and very dry. I took a look in the guest closet for the sheets and they are all in there. No stains on the floor everything was smelling nice and fresh and yes, once again I will say it was squeaky clean.

I took my chance on asking Uncle a question. "Hey Uncle" do you think Uncle Sam is capable of committing an ungodly act? Uncle said," No" not Uncle Sam, "Why do you ask"? What do you think he did? Well after that statement I felt I needed to shut up. No one was going to believe anything I say. Sam really covered his tracks.

A few days went by. Now it's time for Gramps home going service. He had a grand home going service. Gramps had a twenty-one-gun salute. "And can you believe Sam never showed up to Gramps funeral. How do you not pay your last respect to man you have called your brother for over forty years? "What a shit face."

My summer vacation was over. I thank God for all his small favors, this summer. Because to me, when I sit back and look at it from the view point of my God. Those little favors were really big ones. "For real." They were mighty big.

CHAPTER 9

THE TASTE OF HATE

I entered into a different me. A self I never knew could exist with in me. I no longer felt compassion or love. I no longer had fear. Just hate. I no longer had a likeness for people. For the next twenty years I hated the world and everything in it. Every day, every second of my being. Every wakening moment and every breath I took. I would pray that bad things would happen to Sam.

The hate I had for Sam consumed my life for the next twenty years. "Please have a seat", because you're about to read the conversations I had with God and the Devil. You are about to read about my physical, mental and spiritual transformation.

Heavenly Father I am so angry right now. I know right from wrong, and I know my thoughts, my prayers, my wishes and my unforgiving is all wrong. And weather you forgive me or not, I really don't care right now. I have been violated and abandon by all who have promised to protect and love me. I really wish, and I will continue to pray. That Sam die a lonely death and burn in "HELL" "I pray he drops dead", "I pray he gets beat to death". "I pray he gets violated as he has violated me." "I pray he goes to jail and get rapped, a hundred times a day every day."

Whenever I looked into the mirror I saw me as no one else could. I saw red blood dripping from my eyes. I saw my light skin turn charcoal black, each and every day I felt like I was becoming more in human than any boy or girl could ever be.

Today I'm not speaking to God. I'm speaking to Jesus. "Jesus" we are taught to come to you first with our issues," I have no issue, and I just have a request." "I don't want you nor your father to forgive my sins". "I am not asking for forgiveness." "I wish Sam the worst life ever."

You see all of my conversations were always with the Most High. The devil was just sitting there quietly taking over and taking advantage of every moment I asked God not to forgive me. I just wanted Sam to suffer and never ever have an ounce of peacefulness in his life.

The Taste of Hate

A few years has passed a friend of mine I have known since child hood. Yeah I know at this time I'm still a child. I have known her since Kindergarten. We are twelve years old now. I get word from my mother she got hit by a car and later on died. I said to my mother,

"TO BAD FOR HER" My mother looked at me and was in a state of shock.

My mother said she was going to cook some food and we were taking it to her mother's house. We will leave about four o'clock. So get your things together and be ready by four. I said to my mother. I'm not going. The girl is dead so what. My mother did not quite know how to deal with my new found attitude. All she could say was. I will deal with you when I get back. In my head I was like "YEAH RIGHT, WHAT EVER LADY, GO TO HELL"

One night I heard my Grandmother on the phone talking to Miss Delores. If you can remember Miss Delores is Sam's Wife. Miss

Delores and my Grandmother were friend's way before they found their men and got married. Miss Delores was telling My Grandmother how Sam was in the intensive care unit.

How he went out the night before and got drunk with the wrong people. I also need you to remember he liked to gamble. My Grandfather's house was a safe haven for him. The story is he went out to some strange place to gamble. He was shooting craps and playing cards. He got a little too drunk. His gambling crew decided to rob and beat the living shit out of him.

I was listening to my Grandmother tell my mother how they broke his leg cracked his ribs knocked out all of his bottom front teeth. He had to get seventeen stiches in his head." OH MAN" was I happy for the moment. I was "singing and dancing and skipping around the house like I had a bag of candy all to myself. Better yet, I was happier than a bunch of kids in a candy factory. "OH THANK YOU GOD

The Taste of Hate

THANK YOU, THANK YOU, AND THANK YOU.

Lord I am about to say something I know you're not going to like, and right now, again I don't care, and I am not going to ask for your

forgiveness. Because this is how I feel. I hope he drops dead right now. I hope he never makes it out of the intensive care unit. Honestly I don't understand why you just won't let him die."

Now I'm fourteen. I woke up one morning with my tongue feeling like my mouth is now too small. I awake with the feeling of a swollen tongue, a tongue feeling too large for my mouth. Topped with the ruggedness of hard coarse sandpaper coated with hot burning sand straight from the Sahara Desert. As I glided the tip of my tongue across the roof of my mouth from back to front and gently down the back of my front teeth. I felt my tongue slit in two as if it was a fork in the road, and each of those slits were split in two tails. As my tongue left passing my lips I heard the same sounds in my head every day of snakes rattling and hissing. At night when I lay in my bed to sleep and I rub my skin. I feel the ruggedness of a giant reptile. I can feel that I have a long tail, and in my head I can see this tail vividly whipping and lashing all those who would get in my way, or step into my darkness. I could see me beating Sam unmercifully. I can hear him screaming as if I was slowly peeling his skin off his body layer by layer, as he tries desperately to speak, asking me with his ratchet lips quivering the words "please forgive me". 'I'm sorry'. As I reach out to slap Sam in the face, I notice my nails are the nails of a bear. Strong black and deadly.

My conversations with God became more like me telling him what I wanted. And me telling him, I'm all that matters right now. I didn't care what God or anyone wanted of me. Then there were those days where I would wake up after feeling like the devil himself and asking God to bear with me. Because there were

The Taste of Hate

days where all I could and would do is pray for God not to turn his back on me.

Every move, every breath I took was centered on Sam. My hatred for Sam was controlling my life. I had nothing nice to say to anyone. I just wanted to be left alone. You could sit across from me in a conversation. Mentally and spiritually I would be gone. I would be sitting right in your face and not see or hear you. I would see myself in the image of the devil, as I see him.

I had the meanest conversation with God about Sam. Crying because I can no longer taste the joys of life in my mouth. My ice cream would melt and be on fire before I could part my lips. My food taste of burnt ash. Then I had a taste in my mouth that was indescribable. Nothing tasted the same. Every second of the day, every minute in an hour and every hour of the day. All I would do is pray something bad would happened to Sam. My prayers at this time was to Satan.

He didn't deserve to live. He didn't deserve to be loved by anyone. He didn't deserve to have a friend or be a friend to anyone. He needed to die and burn in Hell. He first needed to suffer here on earth.   One who violates a child should not have the right to breathe the same air as any decent person on this planet.

My cousin asks me one day to pick up her crying baby. I ignored her because I knew at that time, no baby needed to feel the negative energy I held. That baby would have been jacked up and emotionally torn down for no reason. That's the way I was feeling. No one good deserved to be inflicted with my state of being. I was in my head saying." You pick your own damn baby up" "I'm not picking up that little mother fucker". I would never go near any child. I was afraid my evilness would be transferred to them.

The Taste of Hate

Every time I would exhale, I could see grey smoke flowing out of my ears. I could feel the heat of flames in my mouth as the black smoke rushes out of my nostrils. As I strolled down the street I could hear myself walk as if I was a giant weighing in at thirty tons. Every day I saw my shadow no matter the time of

day. I saw the shadow of what I had become on the inside. This shadow followed me everywhere. Even in the house. The inside me was trying desperately to escape and fully take over. My inner darkness had already consumed ninety-nine percent of who I use to be. Not only did I hate Sam. I became Hate. I brought hate to life.

My prayer changes a little. "Oh heavenly father my light is almost dim. I beg of you, to not let me go. I'm sorry I am still at a place where I don't want you to forgive me for my thoughts on how I feel about Sam. I ask you today dear father God, please guide me through this. "YES I HATE SAM", YES I WISH HE WOULD DIE A HORRIFIC DEATH! "YES I

PRAY THAT THE DEMONDS OF THE EARTH WOULD ONE DAY SUCK HIM THREW THE MANY LAYERS OF THE EARTH. CRUSHING HIS BONES PIECE BY PIECE, INCH BY INCH AS HE TRAVELS THROUGH TO THE FIREY PIT OF THE EARTH. I WANT HIM TO FEEL HIS BLOOD POUR THROUGH EVRY WHOLE IN HIS BODY. I WANT HIM TO FEEL HIS TOES BEING SNATCHED FROM HIS FEET ONE BY ONE. I WANT HIM TO SEE EACH OF HIS FINGERS DECENERGRATE BEFOR HIS EYES. YES! I WANT HIS TONGUE TO BURST INTO FLAMES. FATHER GOD I DO NOT WANT NOR AM I GOING TO ASK FOR YOUR FORGIVNESS. IF YOU SEE FIT DEAR FATHER TO TAKE AWAY ALL OF MY LIFES BLESSINGS, BECAUSE OF THE WAY I FEEL BECAUSE OF MY WISHES UPON YOUR SON SAM. THEN AT THIS MOMENT I AM WILLING TO SACRIFE IT ALL. I JUST ASK YOU IN THE NAME OF JESUS DON'T LET GO OF MY HAND, EVEN IF IT'S JUST A PINKY. DON'T LET ME GO.

The Taste of Hate

I haven't stepped inside of a church in "years" because I feared I was going to burst into flames the second I stepped past the door.

I got up one morning, I took a shower. And as I was about to get dressed Miss Delores called wanting to speak to my Grandmother.

So I called my Grandmother to the phone and I sat right there in her face, butt naked, all I had has a towel around me. I wanted to hear everything. I knew it was about Sam.

"YES" he had a stroke and he has difficulties in walking and speaking "YES" I jumped for joy. I was crying with tears of joy and happiness in my heart my spirit felt "really good." But he was still alive and for that I was grateful.

Heavenly father please don't let him die, he needs to suffer. Now I'm really afraid of myself. Because now I have hatred with a smile. I had a good day. I was still dark inside. I couldn't eat. I still had a black heart.

Six months later. Sam was trying to walk his crippled ass across the street, he couldn't move fast enough a car knocked the shit of him. He got away with minor bruising and a broken leg. "OH YEAH" I was having another great day.

The more pain Sam was in the better I was feeling. "Thank you Jesus". My black heart and my rotten insides, was seeing a little light. I still saw my shadow; my weight was still three tons. I still had no compassion or love for anyone. I stayed out of site for years. I was just walking through the streets doing what I had to do as if I was invisible to the world.

My Grandmother had no idea what was going on in my shut down world, she was my human kryptonite. I knew at any given time, all I had to do was hug my Grandma, and all the

The Taste of Hate

hatred I had in my core would have fled the earth. I loved my Grandmother more than anyone or anything on this planet. For her to be happy I would give my soul to the devil. My Grandmother was my light on earth. She knew something evil was inside me was brewing for a long time. She knew her grand

baby haven't been her grand baby for years. She just didn't know why.

I got up one morning and laid down in the center of my bedroom floor. My Grandmother came into the room to check on me. When she saw I was on the floor she slowly backed out of the room and closed my door. She returned with a hand full of mustard seeds and poured them all over me. I just laid there in silence. As she stood over me, she said quietly. I love you and God loves you to.

Now I want you to always keep at least one of these mustard seeds with you at all times. Then she handed me the bible. I moved away from the bible because in my state of mind it was going to burn in my hands. The next thing I know my Grandmother sits on the floor besides me and starts to pray. For the devil to free my soul. Only I believed at that time I was the devil. Well maybe a small version of the devil in the making. Her praying to free me had no effect what so ever. I was praying she would get up and leave. So I said to her. GET, OUT, OF, MY, ROOM.

My Grandmother quickly jumps up, and then she stopped, she started flicking through the bible when she found what she was looking for. Grandma placed the open bible on the edge of my bed. To be truthful, I thought my Grandma was going to stomp the shit out of me. Shortly after Grandma leaves my room. I get up to see what she wanted me to read. It was as clear as day and that's because it was underlined in pencil. This is what she left for me to read.

MATTHEW 17:18 AND JESUS REBUKED THE DEVIL;

(In my head as I read it, I said that's what Jesus do. That's not what Hattie Mae does, and it's not what I'm going to do today.)

So I read the next penciled item.

MATTHEW 17:20 AND JESUS SAID UNTO THEM BECAUSE OF YOUR UNBELIEF: FOR VERLIY I SAY UNTO YOU, IF YE HAVE FAITH AS A GRAIN OF MUSTARD SEED, YE SHALL SAY UNTO THIS MOUNTAIN, REMOVE; HENCE TO YOUNDER PLACE; AND IT SHALL REMOVE; AND NOTHING SHALL BE IMPOSSIBLE UNTO YOU.

So basically all I got out of that was all I needed was a dot of faith. My attitude then was, so what I got that, and just like my little bit of faith I took the mustard seed and put it in my pocket. (I know now, not then that my mustard seed of faith is what kept me grounded)

I said to myself: "Not today Granny." I'm still breathing fire out my mouth and I blow smoke threw my nose. As I got myself together. I left my bed unmade, never touching the Bible. I picked up as many mustard seeds as I could scrap together. I put some seeds in the palm of my hand. I go to the kitchen were Grandma is. She's doing what she does, and that's cooking breakfast for everyone. I open my hand and as she looks into the palm of my hand I put the mustard seeds into my jean pants pocket. Grandma smiled and I left out to start my day.

Well a few years has gone by, it's now spring of 1979. I just got home from a long day of work. Wishing it was Friday. As I enter the house my Grandmother was already on the phone. I had no idea at the time who she was speaking to. All I heard was." I'm sorry to hear that". Oh! "My God bless his soul". So I shrugged my shoulders walked toward my room and said to myself. Another death big deal. Then I heard my Grandma say. Ok Delores. I stopped and turned around to my

The Taste of Hate

Grandmother and she looked at me and quietly said. It's over.

I hit the floor like the three tons I felt that I weighted. I was screaming and crying full of joy I was yelling, "thank you Jesus", "thank you lord! "Please have mercy on my soul," "I now come to you and ask you to take back my soul from the darkness" "Oh God thank you". "I just can't ask you to forgive me for embracing the hate." "I do ask that you free me from this darkness." "I ask you heavenly father in your son's name not to ever, ever put hate in my heart again".

As I hit the floor all I hear is aloud "BOOM!" that was me hitting the floor. I became so weak I could see the black spirits of hate flowing up and out of my body. As the spirits of hate was leaving my room got brighter and brighter now all I see is a blinding white light everything is white down to my clothing. At first I panicked, but that was only for a split second. I just laid there I felt the weight of the world lift from my body. I was as light as a pigeon's feather. When I stood up to take a step towards my bed. I couldn't feel the floor beneath me. As I looked down at my feet I could see I was walking on air. When I looked up I could feel me being carried across the room and placed in my bed. It was one big giant hand that I could feel but could not see. I felt at peace I felt like a kid, I felt love and compassion.

The next thing I know I woke up to my Grandmother shaking me awake for work. I just laid there looked into her loving eyes silently crying and just hugging her trying to make up for all the years I missed being hugged by her. And then the phone rings. It's Miss Delores, telling My Grandmother Sam died.

I said to myself: "hold up wait a minute," "what just happened?" My Grandmother comes back into my room and said Sam died in his sleep last night. I shook my head in disbelief confused about how and what just happened. I said; Grandma didn't Miss Delores call you yesterday when I got home from work? And didn't she tell you last night Sam Died? Grandma said no baby. I wasn't here when you got home. In fact, when I got home you where sleep. The devil in hell couldn't wake you up. I smiled at her and said to myself, all it ever takes is a mustard seed, and God will show up every time.

Yes, I started crying all over again, thanking Jesus and praying that no one becomes the emotion of hate. We packed up the following week to send Sam to Hell. Some were sending him home. "HA" That man is going straight to hell where he belongs.

I only went to the funeral to make sure he was dead. Seeing him like that brought joy to my soul. As the service went on I was sitting in the church praying to the Devil. I said in my head: "I sure hope you snatched his soul when it left his body." In fact, I hope you came and snatched his soul out of his body while he was awake and breathing. "Sorry God I have to talk to your fallen son right now." After all we did spend a few years together. I just need this one last moment in conversation with him.

I pray you never ever come my way again in life. "You are Hate; you are evil" Today Devil, I bid you a hearty farewell.

Service is now over. We all stood up while they carried the coffin with Sam in it out the door and his family followed.

"WELL, WELL, WELL" What do you know. 'I am laughing my ass off yet again" I am now rolling on the floor. Sorry it was funny then and funnier now. As they were carrying Sam's body down the long church steps. The pallbearers, yes his son's dropped the coffin. "And I'm still laughing," hold on. "I'm so sorry," but Sam fell out the coffin and rolled down the stairs. Thank you Jesus. Or I should say thank you to the falling Angel. I took that as a sign Sam falling into Hell. You don't need to be in a coffin in hell. Can I get a "Hallelujah! "AMEN"

From that day forward I have never ever used the word hate. To me it was and still is the

name of the Satan. It is such a strong, painful, dark and powerful emotion. Hate is an emotion a feeling that if taken to its highest height can mean you may never ever return to the light. Love does conquer all. And all you need is one grain of mustard seed. God is love, love is faith and you really only need it to be the size of a mustard seed.

Rage: Often makes one think that they have physical super powers. Rage increases high levels of Adrenaline in the body. It makes you very violent and crazy like. Almost like mad dog disease.

Hate: Feeling of intense or Passionate dislike for someone, I still say the definition to hate is the Devil. I was and felt all of that.

DEDICATION

This book is dedicated to all those who are in a state of hate or has ever hated someone and has yet to let it go.

If you are still in a dark place, just yell out to the Lord. Ask him for help, ask to be rescued.

Love One Another.

Love and Hate are the two most powerful emotions in the Universe.

The Children we are, are most often the adults we become. Be good to them and protect them as many as you can.

The Taste of Hate

CHALLENGE: Get some mustard seeds and clear tape. Tape one mustard seed to a piece of white paper and give it to someone that is mean, nasty and most often unkind. Tell them to hold on to a little bit of love until you ask for it back, and just walk way. #mustard seed

Thank you for listening and letting me get somethings off my chest. You are the greatest. Have the best day ever.

Hattie Mae.

www.ingramcontent.com/pod-product-compliance
Lightning Source LLC
Chambersburg PA
CBHW071520040426
42444CB00008B/1729